21st Century
Junior Library

TALKING ABOUT
RELIGION

AnneMarie McClain
and Lacey Hilliard

Topics to Talk About

Published in the United States of America by Cherry Lake Publishing Group
Ann Arbor, Michigan
www.cherrylakepublishing.com

Reading Adviser: Beth Walker Gambro, MS, Ed., Reading Consultant, Yorkville, IL
Book Designer: Jen Wahi

Photo Credits: Cover: © Pressmaster/Shutterstock; page 5: © Drazen Zigic/Shutterstock; page 6: © Rawpixel.com/Shutterstock; page 7 (top left): © Anna Nahabed/Shutterstock; page 7 (bottom left): © GoSlow/Shutterstock; page 7 (right): © Southtownboy Studio/Shutterstock; page 8: Odua Images/Shutterstock; page 9 (top): © Scomputer photo/Shutterstock; page 9 (bottom left): © Irina Wilhauk/Shutterstock; page 9 (bottom right): © saravutpics/Shutterstock; page 10–11: © Mila Supinskaya Glashchenko/Shutterstock; page 12 (left): © SketchJack/Shutterstock; page 12 (right): © BeautifulPicture/Shutterstock; page 13: © LightField Studios/Shutterstock; page 14: © Leo Fitliz/Shutterstock; page 16: © Brocreative/Shutterstock; page 17: © WESTOCK PRODUCTIONS/Shutterstock; page 18 (left): © PRASANNAPIX/Shutterstock; page 18 (right): © shutt2016/Shutterstock; page 19: © grafnata/Shutterstock; page 20–21: © pixelheadphoto digitalskillet/Shutterstock

Library of Congress Cataloging-in-Publication Data has been filed and is available at catalog.loc.gov.

Cherry Lake Publishing would like to acknowledge the work of the Partnership for 21st Century Learning, a network of Battelle for Kids. Please visit *http://www.battelleforkids.org/networks/p21* for more information.

Printed in the United States of America
Corporate Graphics

CHERRY LAKE PRESS

CONTENTS

LET'S TALK ABOUT RELIGION

Religion is a set of beliefs a group of people have. The beliefs can be about how the world works. They can be about the meaning of life. They can be about what people think is right or wrong. They can be about what happens after someone dies.

Some religions have a God or gods. Some do not. For many people, religion is a part of who they are. It can be a part of their family culture and

For many people, religion is part of who they are. It is part of their family and culture.

history. Everyone should be free to have a religion or not.

You might have a religion, or you might not. What someone thinks about religion is called their **religious beliefs**. You may not be sure about your religious beliefs yet. You may not be sure you have any. Religious beliefs can change. People in the same family can have different religious beliefs.

The most common religion in the U.S. is Christianity. There are also many people in the U.S. who are Jewish, Hindu, Buddhist, and many other religions.

Look!

These kids are all practicing different religions. What do you notice? In what ways could these kids be different? In what ways could they be the same?

Some religions have places for people to gather. They may gather at a synagogue, mosque, temple, church, or meeting house. Some people gather at these places often, such as once a week. Others go only once in a while. Sometimes people go to school at religious places.

In many religions, there are important writings or books people learn from. In a religion called Buddhism, there are writings called the Tripitaka.

7

In Christianity, there is a book called the Bible. In Islam, there is a book called the Qur'an. In Judaism, there is a book called the Torah.

Many religions have celebrations, holidays, and special times of devotion. People of the same religion may have shared traditions. They may gather and pray. They may do acts of service to show their faith and help others. People might wear clothes that show their faith. Music and singing can be a part of activities and religious celebrations.

Many people light candles in temples, at shrines, and in churches when they pray.

9

KIDS AND RELIGION

If you have a religion, it may feel really important to you. It may make you feel good. You may enjoy sharing your religion with your family. You may enjoy the traditions of your religion.

If you don't have a religion, you might feel curious about religions. You don't need to have a religion. Anyone can have a religion if they would like. It's a choice each person can make.

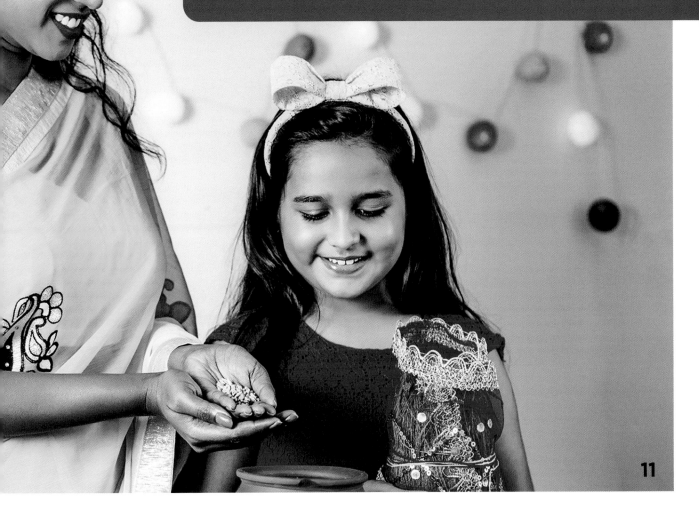

Make a Guess!

What would the world be like if everyone believed all the same things?

11

You can feel good in your own ways. You can do other things with your family.

People sometimes feel strongly about their religious beliefs. Strong feelings can sometimes lead to **disagreements** and hurt feelings. It's always important to show respect for others.

People who practice Judaism consider the Torah a holy book.

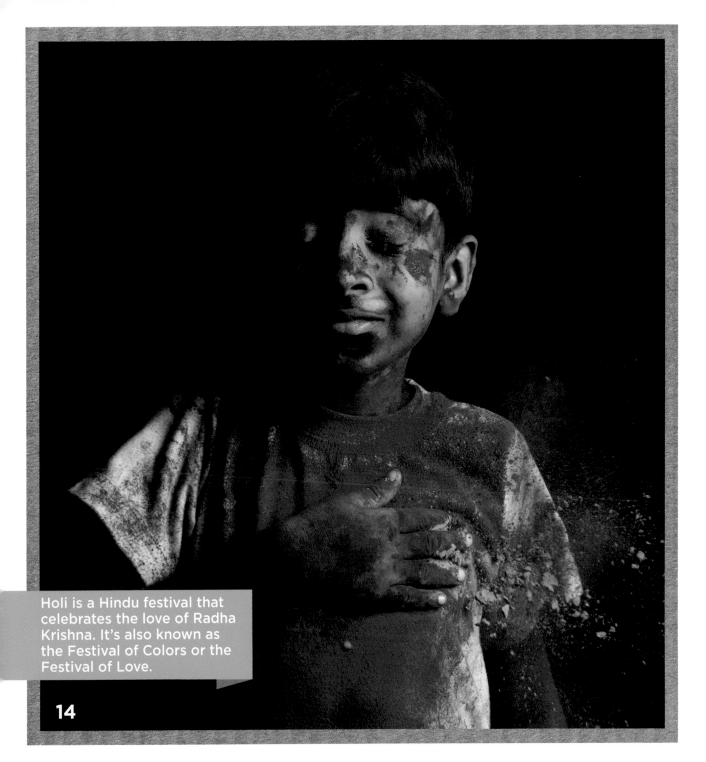

Holi is a Hindu festival that celebrates the love of Radha Krishna. It's also known as the Festival of Colors or the Festival of Love.

WHAT'S MOST IMPORTANT TO REMEMBER?

Religion matters to a lot of people. You can make up your own mind about what you believe. You can also change your mind.

Think!

Does your family have a religion? If so, how do you practice religion in your family? If not, what are some things you do together in your family?

You can talk with others about beliefs. You can talk in ways that show respect for everybody. Knowing about different beliefs helps you understand and show love to people. It's good to be curious about what other people believe.

You can talk to your friends or family about what they believe.

You can learn a lot from people who practice a religion you don't know much about.

REFLECTING ABOUT RELIGION

Are you curious about different religions? Where could you go to learn more about religions?

What can you do to help kids of all religions feel included? What is something grown-ups around you could do to help kids of all religions feel included?

Do you know anyone who practices a different religion than you? What questions could you ask them?

Create!

Come up with a list of questions about religions. Make a plan about how to find the answers.

Ask Questions!

Ask a librarian for help to learn more about different religions. Where do people of different religions gather? What do they do together? What do they believe?

Sometimes, people make decisions based on their religions. They may not eat a certain kind of food or drink or they may do different types of community service. Have you seen these choices or activities based on religions in your community?

21

GLOSSARY

culture (KUHL-chuhr) beliefs, social norms, and values of a group of people

devotion (dih-VOH-shuhn) act of being faithful or dedicated to someone or something

disagreements (dis-uh-GREE-muhnt) having different opinions or feelings from someone else

faith (FAYTH) belief and trust in someone or something, such as a religion

God (GAHD) supreme being worshipped by people in some religions

pray (PRAY) to talk to or connect with someone or something important in a religion

religion (rih-LIH-juhn) system of beliefs and practices

religious beliefs (rih-LIH-juhs buh-LEEFS) things people believe about their religion

traditions (truh-DIH-shuhns) thoughts, actions, and stories commonly accepted by a group of people

LEARN MORE

Book Series: *How the World Worships* by various authors
https://cherrylakepublishing.com/shop/show/52917

Video: National Geographic "Little Kids Big Questions" trailer (2018, ~2 mins)
https://www.youtube.com/watch?v=9aSKic1a53A

Video: BuzzFeed Video - Kids of Different Religions Describe God (2018, ~4:30)
https://www.youtube.com/watch?v=fPYyWhtTDmQ

Various: with grown-up guidance - especially teachers: lesson plans and videos for a variety of grades
      PBS Learning - *Religion & Ethics News Weekly: Access World Religions*
      https://ny.pbslearningmedia.org/collection/awr0

INDEX

ABOUT THE AUTHORS

AnneMarie K. McClain is an educator, researcher, and parent. Her work is about how kids and families can feel good about who they are. She especially loves finding ways to help kids and families feel seen in TV and books.

Lacey J. Hilliard is a college professor, researcher, and parent. Her work is in understanding how grown-ups talk to children about the world around them. She particularly likes hearing what kids have to say about things.